Chinese Australians

Book 1

Australia and China Before Captain Cook

How Trepang, Sea Voyages, and Cultural Exchange linked Australia to Asia

Marji Hill

Published by The Prison Tree Press 2025

Copyright © 2025 Marji Hill

The Prison Tree Press
Suite 124
1-10 Albert Avenue
Broadbeach, Queensland 4218
https://marjihill.com

ISBN 9781763738423 Hardback
ISBN 9781763738430 eBook

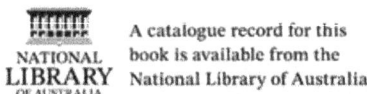 A catalogue record for this book is available from the National Library of Australia

All rights reserved. No part of this book may be reproduced, stored in a retrieval system, or transmitted in any form or by any means, electronic, mechanical, photocopying, recording, scanning, or otherwise, without the prior written permission of the publisher.

Disclaimer:

All the material contained in this book is provided for educational and informational purposes only. No responsibility can be taken for any results or outcomes resulting from the use of this material.

While every care has been taken to trace and acknowledge copyright the publishers tender their apologies for any accidental infringement where copyright has proved untraceable.

Every attempt has been made to provide information that is both accurate and effective, however, the author does not assume any responsibility for the accuracy or use/misuse of this information.

Acknowledgement is given to Canva for most of the illustrations in this book. The paintings, however, were created by Marji Hill.

THE SERIES

Chinese Australians

Book 1

Australia and China

Before Captain Cook

Book 2

Early Chinese Migrants

The First Chinese Australians

Book 3

Chinese and Gold

the Chinese on the Australian Goldfields

Book 4

The Chinese Experience

The Untold Story of Prejudice and Violence on the Australian Goldfields

Book 5

The Chinese Legacy

How Migration, Culture and Community have Influenced Australia

Acknowledgements

I acknowledge the Traditional Custodians
of Country throughout Australia
and their connections to land, sea, and community.

I pay my respect to elders, past, present, and emerging
and extend my respect to all First Nations peoples today.
In the spirit of reconciliation,
my mission is to increase understanding
between the First Nations and other Australians
and to provide people from all over the globe
some basic understanding of Australia s first people,
their history, and cultures.

In addition,
I thank Eddie Dowd for helping me get this book
into its final form for publication.
I also acknowledge the support
from John and Sherien Foley.

Marji Hill

Table of Contents

1. Did the Chinese Visit Australia Long Ago?   1
2. An Ancient Ocean Highway   5
3. What is Trepang?   9
4. The Journey of the Macassans   13
5. Trade and Friendship with First Nations Peoples   17
6. Rock Art Tells the Story   21
7. Why Did It Stop?   23
8. The Trepang Legacy   25

GLOSSARY   29
SOURCES   31

ABOUT MARJI HILL   33
MORE BOOKS BY MARJI HILL   35

1. Did the Chinese Visit Australia Long Ago?

Let us travel back in time—way back several centuries to the early 1400s. During that time, the Chinese were some of the world's greatest explorers. They built huge ships and sailed across vast oceans to explore new lands.

One of the most famous Chinese explorers was Zheng He (1371–1433). Showing the power of the Ming Dynasty, he led a massive fleet of ships on long voyages between 1405 and 1432.

Zheng He's ships travelled to many distant places, including parts of India, Africa, Java, and Sumatra. His fleet also reached the island of Timor, just north of Australia. Since Australia lies only a short distance south of Timor, some people believe that Zheng He and his crew may have seen or even landed in Australia.

But here is the twist: there is no solid proof yet. Historians have not found written records or clear evidence to confirm that Zheng He made it to Australia. Still, it is an exciting idea, and one day more clues might be found.

There are a few interesting hints, though. At the National Museum of Australia, there is mention of a 1477 map that appears to show the outline of the Australian continent. That is more than 300 years before Captain Cook!

Also, British navigator Matthew Flinders noted something curious. He wrote in his journal of the *HMS Investigator* that Australia's First

Nations people in the Gulf of Carpentaria seemed to already know about iron tools and firearms. He also discovered fragments of pottery. He reported seeing pieces of earthen jars, bamboo latticework and other articles which he thought to be of Chinese origin. Could these be signs of early visits from China?

Maybe.

Could the Chinese have visited Australia before Captain Cook?

In 1879, something even more surprising turned up: a small Ming dynasty statue from China was found in Darwin. Around the same location, some porcelain from the same era was also discovered.

These are just clues, though. Most historians agree that the idea of Chinese arriving in Australia before the British is still just a theory, not proven fact.

2. An Ancient Ocean Highway

Before the British occupied Australia in 1788 and set up their first colony in Sydney, Australia was not empty.

Australia's First Nations peoples had lived here for 65,000 years, and there were also visitors from overseas. Some of those visitors were from nearby Asian countries, and they came not to settle but to trade.

Northern Australian coast

For several centuries there had been a trading connection between Australia and China. Macassans from Indonesia came to the northern Australian coast for a period of several hundred years to just after the conclusion of the nineteenth century.

A kind of "ocean highway" existed between the north coast of Australia, southern China, and the Indonesian island of Sulawesi.

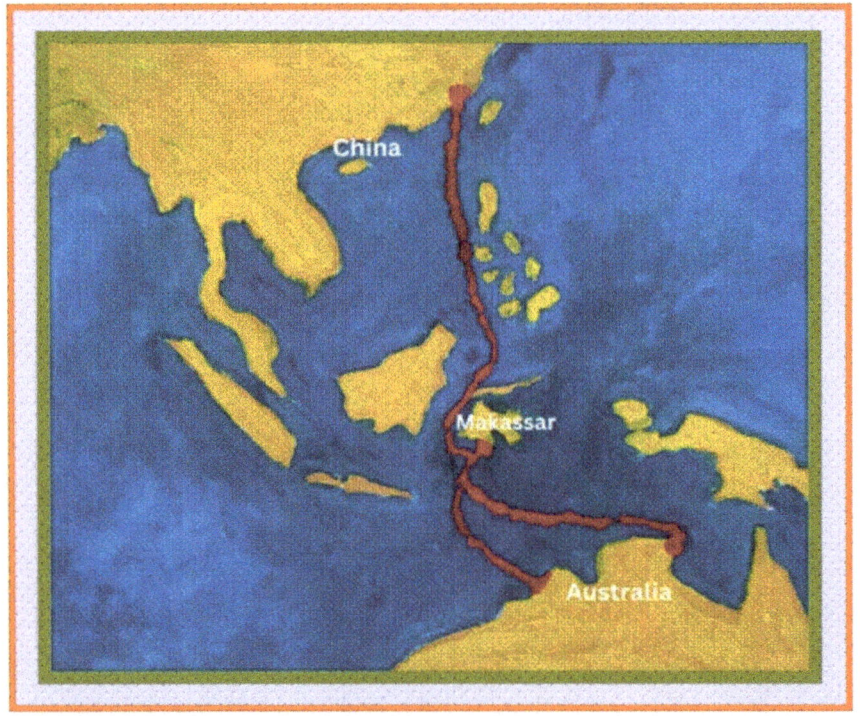

Mud Map - Trade route between Australia and China via Makassar

This sea route made it possible for traders to travel by boat from one place to another. The journey was helped by the winds that blew across the Timor Sea at certain times of the year. These winds made sailing from Makassar (a port town in Sulawesi) to northern Australia much easier.

Note:

The spelling *Makassar* is used when referring to the place and to its people. *Macassan* is an historic spelling referring to the Indonesian fishermen who came to northern Australia.

This ocean highway was part of a larger network of sea trade routes that connected many parts of Southeast Asia. China was a major player in this network. People from countries like Indonesia, the Philippines, and even India were all part of this huge trading system that had been around for centuries.

One of the most important trade items on this route was something you might not expect: a squishy, slimy creature from the sea called trepang.

3. What is Trepang?

Trepang, also known as sea cucumber or beche-de-mer, is a sea animal with a long, soft body and leathery skin. It lives on the sea floor, often in shallow coastal waters. Even though it does not look very appetising to most Australians, it was very popular in Chinese cooking.

Trepang was considered a delicacy and was also believed to have medicinal powers. Some people even thought it could improve health and increase energy or strength.

Trepang

Trepang is still eaten in China today. It is not just food—some people still believe it has healing powers. It is used as a dietary supplement and medicine to treat things like ulcers, high blood pressure, and skin conditions.

Back in the 1800s, about one-third of all the trepang eaten in China came from the northern shores of Australia.

By the late 1600s, the Chinese had a strong appetite for trepang, but supplies near China were running out. As demand for trepang increased, expansion into external markets started in earnest.

The trepang-rich waters of northern Australia

The expansion led to the exploitation of Southeast Asian waters and eventually to the coastlines of Australia and the Pacific Islands. The sea cucumbers near the Chinese coasts were not very high quality. So, Chinese traders began looking for new sources, and that is when the trepang-rich waters of northern Australia became important.

But the Chinese did not come directly. Makassar, situated on the southwest peninsular of Sulawesi in Indonesia, was the centre of a trading network. It was the Macassans who collected the trepang, the largest Indonesian export to China, but the commerce was controlled by the Chinese merchants living in Makassar.

These Macassan visitors became some of the earliest overseas traders to interact with First Nations people.

By the time the British started to occupy the eastern coast of Australia, the trade network connecting Australia to China was in full swing.

4. The Journey of the Macassans

Each year, when the northwest winds began to blow, Macassan fishermen prepared for their long journey.

They set sail from the Indonesian port of Makassar heading south to the coasts of Arnhem Land and the Kimberley region in northern Australia.

Macassan fishing prau

Their journey covered around 1,600 kilometres and usually took 10 to 15 days. At least a thousand Macassans visited northern Australia each year. They came in fleets of wooden boats. This type of fishing boat was called a *prau*.

The Macassans stayed for around five months, gathering trepang and preparing it for sale before sailing home when the winds changed direction.

They set up temporary camps along the coast, close to the shallow waters where trepang was found.

Macassan camp

In these camps, they built stone fireplaces and large cauldrons to boil the trepang. After boiling, the sea cucumbers were buried in sand, smoked, and dried.

The processed trepang was then packed and taken back to Makassar and finally sold to Chinese merchants.

**The Macassans built stone fireplaces
and large cauldrons to boil the trepang**

5. Trade and Friendship with First Nations Peoples

The arrival of the Macassans was not just about collecting the sea slug. It led to hundreds of years of contact between them and the local First Nations communities, especially the Yolngu people of northeast Arnhem Land.

These fishermen were predominantly Muslim.

This contact was not hostile—in fact, it was mostly friendly. The Macassans came back to the same places each year and built relationships with the same families.

The Yolngu traded pearl shells, turtle shells and cypress pine timber.

Over time, the Yolngu and Macassans traded goods. The Yolngu traded pearl shells, turtle shells, and cypress pine timber. In return, they received metal tools, knives, cloth, rice, and tobacco.

The Macassans introduced the smoking of tobacco to coastal First Nations peoples. They used long Macassan pipes.

On these voyages from Asia, they were also a regular source of alcohol, betel nut and possibly opium.

Macassan words crept into the local language as did tools and the making of the dugout canoe.

Dugout canoe

The Yolngu people learned how to use the introduced iron tools, something they did not have before.

Discovering the benefits, they began to manufacture dugout canoes. These were much more stable and seaworthy than the traditional ones made from bark.

Trade with the Macassans would have been one of the main sources of metal for use in shovel-nose spears. This then provided Yolngu with a valuable commodity for trade with other First Nations groups inland.

Some Yolngu people even sailed back to Sulawesi with the Macassans, married into local families, and lived there. This created a deep and lasting bond between the two cultures.

The influence of the Macassans can still be seen today. Many Macassan words are now part of Yolngu languages. Traditional stories, dances, and songs tell of the visitors from the north. And the tamarind trees that grow near the old camp sites? They came from seeds left behind by the Macassans!

Tamarind tree

6. Rock Art Tells the Story

There is physical evidence of this contact with Asia too — you do not have to take just our word for it. Some of the most exciting evidence comes in the form of rock art.

In northern Australia, First Nations artists painted images of Macassan boats, people, and trepang processing.

These artworks are not just decorations. They are like historical records, passed down for generations. They show the clothing Macassans wore, the tools they used, and the friendly interactions between the two groups.

These artworks remind us that the history of Australia did not begin with British colonisation. There were stories, travels and trade long before 1788.

7. Why Did It Stop?

The trepang trade between northern Australia and Makassar continued until the early 1900s.

But in 1907, it came to an end.

Why?

It was probably due to a combination of Australian government policies, such as the introduction of customs duties and fishing licenses, together with the restrictive Immigration Restriction Act of 1901.

Whatever the reason, the Australian government banned the Macassans from returning. This did not just stop the trade—it ended a rich cultural exchange that had lasted for centuries.

The Yolngu were left without important trading partners. They lost access to iron tools, cloth, and other goods. More importantly, they lost long-time friends. Despite this, the memories and traditions of Macassan visits remain strong in Yolngu culture.

8. The Trepang Legacy

Collecting trepang was not difficult. It did not require fancy tools or skills. People could gather it by hand, use spears, or even just feel for them with their feet in shallow water. Once caught, they were boiled, buried, and dried to prepare for the journey back to Asia.

The trade connection that existed between northern Australia and Asia is often forgotten today.

This trading connection which extended from Australia to China demonstrates a sophisticated level of maritime navigation and trade expertise that predates European contact.

Not only goods but new languages, technologies and practices enriched the cultural mosaic of Australia First Nations people.

Trade was a central part of life for First Nations people prior to the British settlement of Australia. This flourishing economy existed with trading pathways crisscrossing the continent dispersing goods, information, technologies and culture thousands of kilometres away from their origins.

These pathways connected First Nations people not only with the entire continent but with the Torres Straits, Papua New Guinea and internationally with Asia.

The seeds of the tamarind tree

The trade connection that existed between northern Australia and Asia is often forgotten today.

But it is a part of our history worth remembering.

This hidden chapter in Australia's history is full of surprising friendships, adventurous sea journeys, and a humble sea slug that helped link two very different worlds.

And best of all?

You now know the story.

GLOSSARY

Arnhem Land – A region in northern Australia home to many First Nations communities.

Beche-de-mer – Another name for trepang.

Delicacy – A special food that is rare or highly valued.

Dugout canoe – A sturdy boat made from a hollowed-out log.

Macassans – Traders and fishermen from the Indonesian island of Sulawesi.

Sulawesi – An Indonesian island where the port of Makassar is located.

Trepang – A sea cucumber, valued in Chinese cooking and medicine.

Zheng He – A famous Chinese explorer from the early 1400s.

SOURCES

The author would like to acknowledge the following sources of information:

Blair, Sandy & Hall, Nicholas (2013) "Travelling the 'Malay Road': Recognising the heritage significance of the Macassan maritime trade route" in *Macassan History and Heritage Journeys, Encounters and Influences* Edited by Marshall Clark and Sally K. May Canberra, ANU E Press, https://library.dbca.wa.gov.au/static/FullTextFiles/924788.pdf

Hill, Marji (2022) *Gold and the Chinese: Racism, Riots and Protest on the Australian Goldfields.* Broadbeach, Qld, The Prison Tree Press. (Gold! Hidden Stories of Australia's Past, Book 3)

Macknight, CC. (1976) *The Voyage to Marege: Macassan Trepangers In Northern Australia.* Melbourne: Melbourne University Press.

Manez, Kathleen Schwerdtner & Ferse, Sebastian C.A. (2010) "The History of Makassan Trepang Fishing and Trade" PLoS One.<https://www.ncbi.nlm.nih.gov/pmc/articles/PMC2894049/#> 2010; 5(6): e11346. https://www.ncbi.nlm.nih.gov/pmc/articles/PMC2894049/

National Museum of Australia. "Early Chinese Migrants". https://www.nma.gov.au/explore/features/harvest-of-endurance/scroll/early-chinese-migrants

Parke, Erin, (2023) "Search for descendants of Aboriginal people who settled in Indonesia at least 150 years ago" https://www.abc.net.au/news/2023-02-11/mystery-community-of-aboriginal-and-indonesian-families/101901188

Ulum, Nurul Bahrul (2021) "Islam in Australia: Historical Links of Aboriginal Australians and Makassar Fishermen" https://mosaicconnections.com.au/islam-in-australia-historical-links-of-the-aborigines-and-makassar-fishermen/

ABOUT MARJI HILL

Marji Hill runs her art career alongside her career as an author. She is a highly respected international author as well as a seasoned business executive, researcher and coach.

Marji is passionate about promoting understanding between Australia's First Nations people and other Australians. The spirit of reconciliation was fostered in all her writings ever since she was a Research Fellow in Education at the Australian Institute of Aboriginal and Torres Strait Islander Studies (AIATSIS) in Canberra.

From 2008 to 2011, Marji was Deputy Chairperson of the Mosman Branch of Reconciliation Australia in Sydney. Following her Research Fellowship at AIATSIS in 1976 Marji, together with her late partner, Alex Barlow, produced more than seventy (70) books on all aspects of the First Nations people including the critical, annotated bibliography *Black Australia*.

In 1989 she was the Project Coordinator and one of the researchers and writers of *Australian Aboriginal Culture* the official Australian Government publication on First Nations people.

In 1988 *Six Australian Battlefields* was published by Angus and Robertson. A decade later it was re-published by Allen & Unwin as a paperback edition. Her nine-volume encyclopaedia, *Macmillan*

Encyclopaedia of Australia's Aboriginal Peoples was published in 2000 and in 2009 she published *The Apology: Saying Sorry To The Stolen Generations*.

Marji's more recent publications extend to self-improvement and self-help with books like *Staying Young Growing Old* and *Inspired by Country* a self-help book about painting with gouache.

MORE BOOKS BY MARJI HILL

First Nations

Hill, Marji 2021 *Australian Aboriginal History: 5 Stories of Indigenous Heroes.* Broadbeach, Qld, The Prison Tree Press.

Hill, Marji 2021 *First People Then and Now: Introducing Indigenous Australians.* 2nd ed. Broadbeach, Qld, The Prison Tree Press.

Aboriginal Global Pioneers

Hill, Marji 2024 *Australian Aboriginal Origins: Earliest Beginnings.* Broadbeach, Qld, The Prison Tree Press. (Book 1)

Hill, Marji 2024 *Australian Aboriginal Trade: Sharing Goods and Services.* Broadbeach, Qld, The Prison Tree Press. (Book 2)

Hill, Marji 2024 *Australian Aboriginal Religion: Country and Dreaming.* Broadbeach, Qld, The Prison Tree Press. (Book 3)

Hill, Marji 2024 *Australian Aboriginal Fire: Managing Country.* Broadbeach, Qld, The Prison Tree Press. (Book 4)

Hill, Marji 2024 *Australian Aboriginal Medicine: Caring for People.* Broadbeach, Qld, The Prison Tree Press. (Book 5)

Self-improvement/Self-Help

Hill, Marji 2014 *Staying Young Growing Old*. Broadbeach, Qld, The Prison Tree Press.

Hill, Marji 2020 *How Big Is Your Why? An Author's Guide to Time Management and Productivity to Achieve Transformational Results*. Broadbeach, Qld, The Prison Tree Press.

Hill, Marji 2020 *A Create and Publish Toolbox: 101 Prompts In A Guided Journal To Help You Write, Self-publish, And Market Your Book on Amazon*. Broadbeach, Qld, The Prison Tree Press.

Hill, Marji 2021 *Inspired by Country: An Artist's Journey Back to Nature, Landscape Painting with Gouache*. Broadbeach, Qld, The Prison Tree Press.

Hill, Marji 2024 *Australian Paintings: Artworks by Marji Hill*. Broadbeach, Qld, The Prison Tree Press.

Gold

Hill, Marji 2022 *Gates of Gold: The Discovery of Gold, its Legacy and its Contribution to Australian Identity*. Broadbeach, Qld, The Prison Tree Press.

Hill, Marji 2022 *Shadows of Gold: Eureka and the Birth of Australian Democracy*. Broadbeach, Qld, The Prison Tree Press.

Hill, Marji 2022 *Gold and the Chinese: Racism, Riots and Protest on the Australian Goldfields*. Broadbeach, Qld, The Prison Tree Press.

Hill, Marji 2022 *Ghosts of Gold: The Life and Times of Jupiter Mosman*. Broadbeach, Qld, The Prison Tree Press.

Hill, Marji 2022 *Blood Gold: Native Police, Bushrangers & Law and Order on the Goldfields.* Broadbeach, Qld, The Prison Tree Press.

www.ingramcontent.com/pod-product-compliance
Lightning Source LLC
Chambersburg PA
CBHW041218240426
43661CB00012B/1083